A FIELD of COLORS

A Children's Book by

Ms. Keita

A FIELD OF COLORS

Ms. Keita

ACKNOWLEDGMENTS

I would like to thank the Holy Spirit for inspiring the vision, words, and manifestation of His talent through me!

P.S. How could I forget acknowledging Zoë Life Publishing

A FIELD OF COLORS

DEDICATIONS

I would like to dedicate this first book to my only son, Quincy Phillips, Jr. As your mother, I will always support, love and honor you. I am grateful to have you as my son.

A FIELD OF COLORS

Ms. Keita

BEAUTIFUL
COLORS

Float around.
Around,
and
round
WITHOUT
a sound.

A FIELD OF COLORS

everywhere I go. The more I see, the more I know!

Red and yellow, GREEN AND BLUE. ORANGE, BLACK, PINK, AND PURPLE TOO!

When you mix them,
more colors will
form.
Bright and dark,
cozy and warm.

Everywhere I turn colors are near me.

When I close my eyes and in my dreams.

UP AND DOWN *and in and out.* Over and under, *beautiful* they are without a doubt.

Colors on my *left* and colors on my *right*. Colors in the *daytime* and colors at *night*.

A RAINBOW OF COLORS OH HOW SO *PRETTY.* THEY ARE NON STOP AND NEVER ENDING!

BEAUTIFUL
COLORS

**Float around.
Around,
and
round
WITHOUT** a sound.

Spring
TIME

- Ms. Keita

Pretty flowers
bloom in
the Springtime.

Rain
falls
on
my
round
face...

The yellow sun shines all around.

Wind blows from place to place.

Springtime is beautiful.

It's a time of peace.

Joy and laughter is in the air.

It's great fun and
good to see.

ABOUT THE AUTHOR

Lakeita K. Phillips is a 2003 graduate of Jackson State University where she earned her B.S. Degree in Childcare and Family Education. She is a teacher, a writer, and is very passionate about being an inspiration in the lives of others. She has worked with many youth, from birth to teenagers beginning in 2003. This is her first published children's book and hopes to write and publish many more in the future.

www.ingramcontent.com/pod-product-compliance
Lightning Source LLC
LaVergne TN
LVHW072104070426
835508LV00003B/263